A SLEEP OF
DROWNED

A Sleep of Drowned Fathers

DONALD ATKINSON

Paintings by Polly de Falbe

PETERLOO POETS

First published in 1989
by Peterloo Poets
2 Kelly Gardens, Calstock, Cornwall PL18 9SA

ISBN 1 871471 04 4

British Library Cataloguing in Publication Data
Atkinson, Donald
  A Sleep of Drowned Fathers.
  I. Title
821'914

  ISBN 1–871471–12–5

Printed in Great Britain by
Latimer Trend & Company Ltd, Plymouth

ACKNOWLEDGEMENTS

Section 1 of *A Sleep Of Drowned Fathers*—the poem beginning "Wailing begins at the house-wall. . ." previously titled 'A Millstone'—won joint 1st Prize in the 1988 *Times Literary Supplement & Cheltenham Festival Poetry Competition* and was published in *The Times Literary Supplement*.

The photographs of Polly de Falbe's original paintings (oil on canvas) were taken by Stephen Oliver.

WITH THE ASSISTANCE OF

SOUTH WEST ARTS

Supported by

Cornwall
County Council

PETERLOO POETS:
Recipient of an Arts Council incentive funding award for 1988/89.

Concerning ancestors, beyond the cosmetic caution against reporting ill of them, stands the weightier imperative that we remain on speaking terms. And there, as Auden said, poetry is our only means of communication: the language in which we come nearest to speaking the truth to each other.

In primitive society, the ancestor is the link between the living and the supernatural.

Contents

A SLEEP OF DROWNED FATHERS

page

On sundran

In Lancashire, by Lune's cow-trodden margins,
where stones were good for skimming the broad shallows,
I found your family grave and you not in it.
Not even your name on their chill marble.
You're safely forgotten in Kent,
drowned by the Motorway.
My mother's somewhere-else-again
and like you on her own.
When we go up there
the sky's unkind,
Northern,
and things aren't right.
There are old mine-workings
('sub*si*dence' she would say)
headstones keep falling in,
she might not even be there.
We leave the flowers
on the spot where we last saw her.

I wonder can this sort of thing
be expected in Kent?
There are coalfields in Kent,
militant once.
If this were to happen to your grave now,
might you find yourselves
suddenly less asunder,
ourselves less sundered in you?

There is talk of an old level
where distant workings connect.
If by a fall
I could bring you there,
would you sink so low?
I'll under you then,
kick out the props—
my hand, take it.
And hold hard, as we fall down the rise.

9

1

Wailing begins at the house-wall where as a child
I would rust lips kissing the rough brick dado,
rub my forehead on it till it bled, then
falling to bruised knees drag down brailled fingers' ends
through a crumble of mortar till my mother called:
stop eating the house, it's dirty!
Adding an anal phoneme—'a'a (caca, shit.)

Indoors she feeds the mangle endless lasagne of washing,
worries because I'm rising three and haven't talked,
busy myself instead with dumb flowers, or seek
identity through injuries. In the sagging
romper-suit she's knitted me (there was a photograph)
I climb the bandy pylon legs of the cast-iron mangle,
feel out its leprosy of blistered green paint.
My mother on the blind side plunges away with the wheel.
When my fingers minced in the cogs' teeth, the pain
froze in my throat and she went on turning
till I fell to the floor with blood enough to
soak the towel she wrapped my shredded hand in.
Our doctor pudged it back to shape and wondered at my
   dumbness.
But I had more than that to shut my mouth on then.

A sister came. We bathe her, my mother and I,
in the rough zinc tub by the fire. First
sample the water with lemon elbows, then gently
immerse our ecstatic pink dough. When we soap her tum
her limbs weave little epilepsies with the air,
her buttocks cradled in the hand are like a stiff hot jelly.
My mother lets me fingertip the pulse
where the bones of the skull haven't closed yet.
For a moment I touch the soft spillable life so thinly sealed.
Who would not want to be her mother? I did.
Or with her in those waters still.

Were we breast-fed? I can't remember it. Only how
from the first dither of an eyelash, Dad, you
hung over us like an axe. Smacked us to sleep.
They say my sister died in your vigils. Six months
breathed under your hand, skin-crazed with eczema.
Each night you turned her onto her sore side,
and when she cried at that you slapped her face.
This was our Margaret and you unleaved her.

2.

There was a way we had to lie that pleased your demons:
head sideways on the pillow, hands folded in prayer
under one cheek, legs yanked out coffin-straight, the feet
laid instep on instep like a little wall. Rigid in bed
we hardly breathed. To ease an itch was sin.

Through the curtained light of our too-early bedtimes
you came like a holy thief, leaving your shoes outside,
walking stiff in stockinged feet on cracked linoleum.
Gaunt, preposterous, soured by a dry religious flame,
handsome you stood on sentry-go at our bedside.
We felt you there and strained to keep our eyes shut.
Inexorably came the spasm of nictation,
and then your hand struck lightning—get to sleep!

"I always aim to miss," he said "the eye itself."

You'd feign departure, fiddle with the door-knob
and tiptoe back. Thinking you gone at last, I'd crack
the seal of an eyelid, glimpse light wet-meshed in lashes,
then your fierce hatchet-face, those eyes like stones,
the hand coming down like a hawk
and the splatted blood-burst of pain
as it landed.

You'd keep this up for hours.
Fear stretched like a rubber-band waiting to snap
that rooted in my eye.
Hooked on the other end, you pulled and pulled.
The thin brown vein diluted, pale as a blonde hair,
tight like wire.
It was bound to break, but when?
Fordoomed to be caught out as well as hurt,
we never learned to lie the way you liked.

3.

Mealtimes were angry with metaphors.
Cut it out!
Cut what out?
Don't answer back. Cut it out, d'you hear!
At six years old the question was where
should we make the incision, which bit mutilate first.
The eye that offendeth, perhaps, that they talked of in Chapel.
Wipe that smile off your face!
An imagined hand reached for a flannel.
Watch out! Or I'll make you smile
on the other side of your face!
I wondered
did you mean you'd knock it sideways, set it straight,
was I smiling left-handed perhaps?
Or would it go
smash through the thickness of my skull,
like the name in Brighton Rock,
till my head became
a huge suckable lump of solid smile.
Was that what they called a gobstopper?
My brother said he thought the smile
would be struck so hard
it would spin right round to the back
and judder in its socket
like hitting the jackpot—gedoinng!
A hairy grin would arrive like an affrit
on the back of my neck
and wobble above my collar-stud.
It would make my mother jump right out of her skin.
I tried to picture her without it:
I could manage the skin without her—
like dropped nylons, I thought—
but a flayed Mother. Would I ever see that?
Had anyone ever seen that?

Language knew of such things.

I'd be eating my cornflakes—
STOP!
You're not breathing properly.
What?
Don't say 'what.' Breathe through your nose.
But I am.
Don't answer me back. You're breathing through your cornflakes;
now breathe correctly, through your nose.
But you knew. You knew I couldn't,
bunged up with adenoids, catarrh, what else.
Breathe properly!
Only my mother's fury in-
hibited your hand, itching to thump the mastoid.

As we sauntered home from the Sunday School you
    superintended,
Walk properly! you'd bellow from behind.
I am.
You're not. You're skipping! Walk properly.
When you explained how to do it,
'Put one foot in front of the other,'
it sounded barmy, how could we not be doing it?
Oh but we could, we could.
From cock-crow to cock-crow
you played O'Grady Says with everything we did—
Stand up! Sit down! O'Grady says knees bend!
We always got it wrong, and all our lives
O'Grady jerks us from behind, plucking at nerves.

On Sunday nights, for a treat, an upside-down Christ,
you'd smear our eyes with spittle to help them stay shut.
It was cold when it came, on your fingers.
And grey I guessed.
I wondered,
were you trying to make us go blind;
or did you wish that we had not been born?

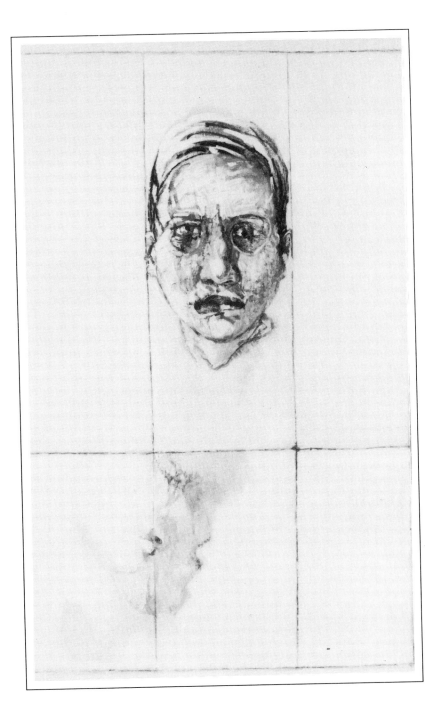

4.

There was a photograph of her, with one of you,
stood either end of the sideboard, flanking a fruit-bowl.
Costumed for *Patience* how beautiful you seemed then.
You, almost the Trevor Howard of *Brief Encounter*;
my mother dark-eyed, raven-tressed, from a different film.
We never found out what went wrong between you. Only
as we grew older and always too early to bed,
while daylight drained from the curtains we listened as you row'd.
In those wars, she was our Joan of Arc before Orleans.
We could hear her defending us, mounting hot charges
against the cold fortifications of your dogma.
And you like a ship beleagered, somehow adrift
from your old moorings in her heart, Quixotic, doomed,
swept by the wildest notions, flagging the impossible.

At last, sounds of a chair falling over,
scuffle of shoes scraping for a foothold,
coughs, cries, sobbing.
And then, once more,
like waves on a shingle beach
the recurring tirade of raised voices,
grating of will against will,
the sound of two rights making wrong.
It happened nearly every night—

except for air-raids; then we felt safer.
Sometimes you'd put the wireless on,
there'd be a concert from the Albert Hall, perhaps.
My Mum would go out half-way through to wash up supper.
You'd sing along, sharing the tenor line with Heddle Nash.
We never heard him. At the end, when the clapping came,
you'd go berserk, rush to the kitchen door—"Ethel!
Just hark at that!" you'd bellow, "Ethel, can you hear that?"
Never impressed, she'd clatter her plates in the sink
while you charged back to the set, turned up the volume
and roared "Hark at them, Ethel, just hark at them!"

The days when you tried to be nice it always went wrong.
You cut loose with a hose-pipe once, us in our school clothes.
Squirting away like a fireman
you came at us through the French windows,
chased us upstairs.
Furniture soaked, living-room carpet wet-through,
us in hysterics, you like an armed clown;
till my mother came back from next-door.
"Trust you, to make an exhibition of yourself!"
she said.

Perhaps you only needed some encouragement.

And that time when, dressed up as Widow Twankey
for the Sunday School pantomime, to make them laugh,
you kicked a football into the congregation
and hit a baby.

5.

Once came War with a kind face and took us away North.
We left you behind to fight the fires of London.
Eight weeks we stayed, in your parents' lime-washed cottage,
its walls like lumpy icing on a cake,
slate floors and creaking stairs, our bedroom windows
tucked under martin-haunted eaves,
a narrow garden perched above the lane,
its lawn rife with permitted daisies,
and a barn with chickens.
At the end of the path a lavatory called Blackpool.

Where's Grandad?
He's gone to Blackpool.
What for?
On private business
(they called it 'business')
we never took long over it.
The fumes of the quicklime we heaped on our Number Twos
could burn the skin off your bum if you hung about.

All night the beck in flood roared past the yard gate
as we dreamed of finding the place where the hens hid their eggs
in the itchy hayloft.
By first light
Grandma crossed us the road
and there from a well
we drew sweet water in a wooden bucket.
Twice a day, our milk
shot straight from the udder into the brown jug.
They sent me for it once
to the farm over the stream.

Shuffling blind on the wet planks,
my nose to the mouth of the quart pot,
I sniffed the warm insides of the cow.
Riffled shadows, alder-shaded,
slid by the corner of my eye.
An ouzel twitted on a stone.

Then
"Walk properly!"
You weren't there but I heard you clear enough,
my foot slipped
and I crashed down, cutting a hand.
The jug broke,
milk and a little blood
poured thinly through gaps in the planks
to be swealed away with the stream.

"He ought never t'ave been sent," said Grandma,
the boy's not used to it."
"Cack-handed," my mother said, and pulled a face.
That sound again—Acko they called me at school.
Acko, quacko, caca fuego, ack-ack.
I pictured you circled in fires, guns cracking shit
as the bombs fell all round and none of them hit you.

In the end you came anyway.
How thin you looked beside my grandfather.
And ill.
Excess of anger, anguish, breeds acid in the gut.
It did for your duodenum. Dad.
You appeared at the stair-foot one grey morning,
hand trembling on the thumb-latch,
your lips morgue-pale,
pyjama-flies gaping, your doings fallen out
like a miniature disembowelling.
Oh help me Ethel! you cried,
help me to get down the garden.
Before they carried you back you'd passed a quart of blood.

We all went back to London then and damn the bombs.
When the hospital sent you home, my mother
nursed you like a lamb, and I wished you'd be
ill more often.

Every few years,
like a comet or rare orchid,
your ulcer burst into flower,
the intestine
peeling its crimson glove onto the white bedsheet.
Was it wrong to think you might have learned from this—read
not a portent but a lesson from this menstruum,
exfoliation of anguish, this woman-flux?

6.

Midday back from Chapel waiting dinner.
You in your Sunday suit, hair quiffed and brilliantined,
thrashing my brother for nothing.
He'd seen a milk-top on the floor and left it there.
My mother in with a knife for the meat, Stop hitting that boy!
It's got nothing to do with you, keep out of it!
You're hitting that boy for what's nothing to do with him.
I know what I'm doing.
Yes, and I know it too.

The line of her thyroid incision burned like a weal.

You can't tell me that boy's done anything to deserve this
on a Sunday.
Keep out of it, you don't know what you're on about.
I'm on about last night.
Last night? What d'you mean, 'last night'?
You're taking it out on that boy because of last night,
aren't you, you mucky hound!

As she pulled at your Sunday clothes her face was burning,
I thought she would die if it didn't stop.
A waistcoat button had torn, she had hold of your silk tie.
You lunged at her clumsily:
Leave me alone, get your hands off!
Why don't you carve the meat?
Carve the meat? That's your job you tripe-hound,
if you did but know it!

Her nose was bleeding, she called out 'Son!
for heaven's sake come and help me, can't you!'

Still dressed from Chapel, in polished shoes
I kicked at your calves from behind. Keep off!
Keep off, or I'll knock you flat!
and you swung me round. From below,
your Adam's apple looked swollen, plucked,
as I reached up and punched you in the throat.

41

Your kick sent me flying, my Mother screamed,
waving the knife in her fist, Don't you dare hurt that boy!
pushing you into the hall.
Did you see that! you bawled
as you backed away up the staircase,
slipping, bumping,
You all saw her go for me with the knife.
I'll give you knife, she sobbed, blood on her face and hands.
Just don't take it out on those children, or I'll give you knife.

7.

I saw an art-thing once, Rauschenberg did:
impaled a seagull to his bed and painted it;
coated the lot—blankets, pillow—in hospital green
and hung it.
Concealed in a mattress somewhere, a tape
dribbled out strained mewtings of Stockhausen
like juice of gallstones.
Oh—
I could have nailed you to your pillow
and hanged you on a wall.
But in my dream
the mark on your throat seemed tired and blue.
It hung there swollen,
sagging,
like a wattle.
For a moment I thought it would fall off,
and reached out a hand to prevent it.

I would not for my life have seen it fall.

8.

In the end she took us away
and we lived on your pence
in the grimy but vivid North.
Dragged apart at last,
we became happy and you got rich.
Between you we didn't meet for fifteen years.

At night, Europe's top man in Steel,
admitted by voice-print, you rise
to air-conditioned luxury in Mayfair.
Key-money on your flat would buy our house outright.
Sundays, in Knightsbridge and Westminster,
ogled by choir-girls of middle age,
still you sing your sacred solos:
Mendelsohn, Handel, always The Lost Chord.
At fifty-five, on half an intestine,
you're given the lead in all God's musicals.

At last, in time of Profumo,
I come to root you out in your fur-lined eyrie.
We talk, but something's frozen between; our words
fall as crystals on the carpet, loth to melt.
You perch, a slick seagull on your chromium chair,
while the iron sleeps in my soul.
I mean to forgive.

Sometimes you send us tickets for the Garden.
We sit in the best seats, the singing's very good,
but you don't cry 'Hark at them, Ethel' any more
when the applause breaks out.

We say we'll keep in touch.

9.

Close of my thirty-second year from you: my birthday.
In the garden I try to outpaint Jackson Pollock.
Underground trains come to the surface here,
bob-sleighing down through the cutting,
slashing the balsam poplars
with streaks of muddied red my dripping brush can't catch.
Indoors, someone's washing her hair.
Wigged in shampoo, her face at the window,
mouthing the word 'Police'.
There's been an accident,
you've had a fall or something.
We go, my brother and I,
and learn from the C.I.D.
how you managed to die on my birthday.
A fall they said:
image of stone steps down to a cellar,
window-ledges, ladders.
But as the man said,
it wasn't like that.
There'd be an inquest.

10.

This was the room: high-ceilinged, vast, festooned
with pulleys, hooks, chains, trapezes, belts, harness.
Atelier fit for Stubbs, draughtsman of horseflesh,
to hammock in bedsheets his huge, stinking cadavers
straining by candlelight to trap their glistening
musculature before the meat fell off,
rainbowed in its cloud of blowflies. Here,
fortnightly, he came to take his pleasure.

The woman led him in; while he undressed
took from the suitcase he'd brought with him
stockings, suspender-belt, panties, bra,
a pair of high-heeled shoes, a feather-hat,
some make-up. Helped by her hands, he drew
those woman-skins over his ailing manhood,
put on the hat, and turning to the wall
looked at himself in the mirror. Inside
the skins he felt both less and more a man;
frisson of rape, frisson of suicide.

Madam seemed clothed from head to foot in shite:
brown shoes brown stockings brown tweed skirt brown tie
and a brown hat, so tightly clamped over her
bobbed cut, they must have banged in rivets
to fix it to her skull in the green wood.
She brought him to it then. His hand in hers
like a tenderfoot kid at the ice-rink
he tottered and sawed his way across the floor
in the high heels, till she steadied him
exactly in the centre of the room,
crossed over to a handle on the wall,
began to turn, and lowered through the air
tagliatelli of leather straps till stopped
full in his fizzog, spilled like entrails.
Cockling for balance on one high heel
he raised a stockinged leg for her to take.

With her other hand she fetched down a loop
from the rigging and wrapped it round. In turn
he lifted the other leg, then both his arms
and waited while she pulled the bindings tight.

In leather cummerbunds she swathed his trunk
and, for his stretched neck, drew down a metal
collar, inches deep, once used for slaves.
He bent his head, she locked it on. Then hooked
it to its chain. Back at the wall, two turns
and the line pulled taut, lifted him off the ground.
He cried out, and she eased him cog by cog
down, till he stood on his heel-toe-tips. Then,
plucking at elbows, she spun him round,
the hat slid off and as the girl came in
his image in the mirror on the wall
flapped a gauche Charleston. Madam pressed a switch.
A tape played Bizet's *Carmen* for the strip.

The hired girl dances closer, flicks her skirt,
her lolly tongue, holding her eyes away—
he pays to look at her, no need to look at him—
enacts her slow tease, peeling off lingerie
like infected dressings, flings them in his face,
his nose and mouth yashmak'd in fetish-kiss.
Nude now, her cold skin stippled newsprint,
stale choreography contorts her shape to
cliché, defines her in the parts that count:
lymphatic buttocks, halo-ed tits, extruded
cunt. Her climax, aimed to achieve his,
to turn, touch toes, and using both hands
open her arsehole at him.
                                        Having done,
drops to all fours, scoops up her clothes and leaves.

Madam returns to feel his crotch. It's dry,
and all's to do still. Tightens several straps,
and kneels to her employment.

It takes
a while. At last he yields a little milk.
She swallows that, and puts it on the bill.
Charges the Cabinet rate, same as for
Party leaders. Like them, he'll afford it.

In a kitchen somewhere the girl has made
a pot of tea. Pours three cups and sugars one.
With slouch of a tired waitress, brings it in,
hands it to him where he hangs, and leaves with
her employer. They'll drink theirs at ease
in the kitchen, over a cigarette.
Give it five minutes, then they'll take him down.

It's Japanese, the way he holds the saucer
with its rattling cup: the pose; that haunted
bird-like stare of the actor in the Noh thing
who plays the Madwoman. As if the grief
were painted onto bone. Or Onan-Narcissus
wept for the self drowned in his own semen.

He drinks with difficulty from the cup;
the priestly collar thwarts him, head must move
in one piece with the trunk, from the knees almost.
He leans back, and the tea slips down his throat
like a warm glove inside. Spills a little
on his chin. Wipes it. Tries to read the leaves
stuck round the rim. Spies in the well of the cup
a sugared brown mouthful still unstirred,
die letzte Süsse. Leans back as before,
this time too far, his foot slides out from under,
one high-heeled shoe flies off, the other breaks,
hangs by a silver toe-strap. His legs begin
kicking that Charleston again, stylishly now
as he pirouettes inches clear of the floor.
The chain pulls on the collar, yanks up
the back of the head, forcing the chin down.

51

Teeth grit on the rim of the cup, it cracks off
and the other hand's waving the saucer,
he's choking on sweet tea as the yoke
cuts off the wind-pipe crushing the Adam's apple.
He loses breath until his heart gives way,
the frantic limbs quieten, swing to and fro
at the end of their tether, a shoe-heel
scraping the floor as the pendulum slows.

To bleeding hells at length they brought him down,
unwrapped the bindings from the swaddled limbs,
broke off the hangman's collar from his neck,
picking out broken china from his teeth,
and with reluctant lips
gave him a kiss of life that came too late.
Then, in a frenzy, dead man on the house,
unraped him of his woman-skins, washed off
the oils of make-up from his eyes and lips,
put the clothes back in the suitcase, and smartly
re-dressed him for the Office.

The rest was cover-up. And failed of course.
The mark on your neck betrayed them.
                                    But then—
nothing ever happens to these people,
why should it? As the coroner said: they
only render a service.
                    Father forgive.

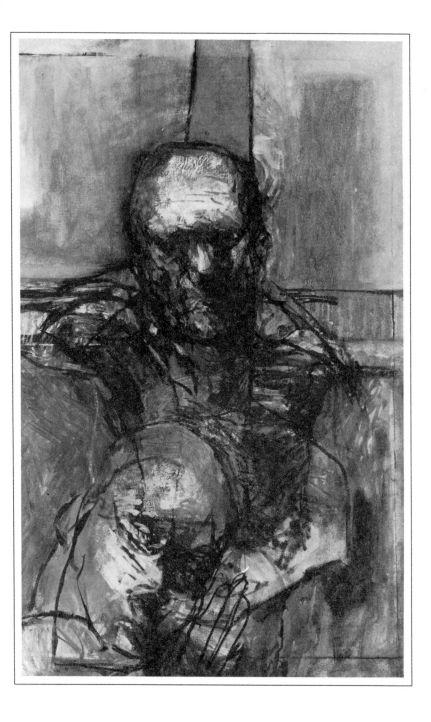

11.

The edge of the tomb cuts off their lower halves,
they rise from behind it or out of it,
one on each side pressing him forward.
The woman puts up her face to him, almost
resting her chin on his shoulder,
where noses, cheeks and lips play mirror-touch.
Their eyes are dreaming one another's sleep.
His arm looks broken; she cradles the nerve-
less elbow in the angle of her own.

The ephebe is looking away, his mouth
falls open and the eyes roll skyward. Is he
singing, way up there in the sinuses?
Off-shoot of his ecstasy, the long
musician's fingers riffle the man's flesh,
the spread hand seeking a chord or a pain,
his arm sleeved in a blue of cornflowers.

Between them the woman and the boy
bear up the torso of the injured man:
athletic, equine, gold of his flesh
exhausted by the olive light, shadowed
with grays of the sky and the marble tomb.
The head with its thorns is a burned sunflower;
coiled shavings of bronze spring down his neck.

There are several wounds, like craters
with a dark spot at the pit, beginning
to glaze over. He's a map of holes, a
constellation of wounds turning in space,
its axis falling from the crown of thorns
down through the bone-gates of the clavicle
the inner arcs of the breasts, the round stone
of the navel, to find its fathom where
like the Venus his concealing hand
hangs at the slack drop of an arm, and the
fingers curl, hiding the place. Just there

the back of the wrist leans out, fractures
the frail proscenium of art. Touch me
it seems to say, as I touch and am touched.

And now,
drawn by complicity of sex and pain,
through the soft female stigmata impressed or
embossed on the equine body of the male—
the nipples, the empty nail-holes, the navel
with its little hill, the open slit—here
in the Brera, Milan, before Bellini,
I reach out hands to you dead Father. Dad.
For there, where their imagined axis runs
like a vertical spit from the thornflower
down through the map of wounds to the sad place,
I see yon' shadowy stranger, your un-
companioned form, pivoting back and forth
like some ghostly escapement; the plumes
of your hat feather the air above the
sacred head; and a single high-heeled shoe
scrapes on the surface of the tomb, as you
turn gently among the wounds.

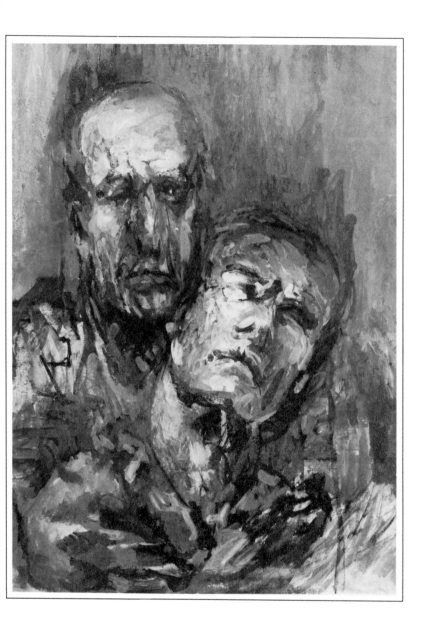

It were better for him

Arms flung round your bruised neck like a charm,
I drag you down, through spirals of thickening
waterlight, to the ocean's utmost floor.
There, like the buried-at-sea enchained,
I rock you 'in the cradle of the deep'—
someone's favourite ballad, was it yours?
We're lapped by lilt of tides, cat-lick of the moon's
tongue on our eyelids, open-and-shut. Eyes
of chrysoprase at the ebb closing, wide-
staring at the full. It's my love, you know
that keeps us here like this, not punishment.
I'll see your bones coralled yet, those eyes made pearls.
The brittle fish that swim this bowl of tears
are working on it. See, your flesh gives
under my weight, you're starting to dissolve.
Will it take a thousand years, the seas run dry
or I turn to stone by this labour?
When the day comes, go decently disguised.
Confused in grains of sand, slip through my
fingers dregs of you unrecognised:
so my dust bites not your last as it goes.
Salt of the sea will change you. Yellows to brown,
purples to green, crimsons to blue: you'll be
rainbowed elsewhere and different. I here,
a millstone son, condemned to lie, till
alkahest of mercy solve this hard love.